EXTREME!

Fried!

When Lightning Strikes

Kay Barnham

Capstone
press

Mankato, Minnesota

Fact Finders is published by Capstone Press,
a Capstone Publishers company.
151 Good Counsel Drive, P.O. Box 669,
Mankato, Minnesota 56002.
www.capstonepress.com

First published 2008

Produced for A & C Black by

Monkey Puzzle Media Ltd
The Rectory, Eyke, Woodbridge
Suffolk IP12 2QW, UK

Library of Congress Cataloging-in-Publication Data

Barnham, Kay.
   Fried! : when lightning strikes / Kay Barnham.
      p. cm. -- (Fact finders. Extreme!)
   Includes bibliographical references and index.
   Summary: "Presents the science of lightning and
   thunderstorms, including dangers and safety
   precautions"--Provided by publisher.
   ISBN-13: 978-1-4296-3121-1 (hardcover)
   ISBN-10: 1-4296-3121-X (hardcover)
   ISBN-13: 978-1-4296-3141-9 (softcover)
   ISBN-10: 1-4296-3141-4 (softcover)
1. Lightning--Juvenile literature. 2. Thunderstorms--
Juvenile literature. I. Title.

QC966.5.B37 2009
551.56'32--dc22

2008027663

Editor: Cath Senker
Design: Mayer Media Ltd
Picture research: Shelley Noronha
Series consultant: Jane Turner

This book is produced using paper that is made from
wood grown in managed, sustainable forests. It is natural,
renewable, and recyclable. The logging and manufacturing
processes conform to the environmental regulations of
the country of origin.

Printed in the United States of America

Picture acknowledgements
Alamy p. 22 (A.T. Willett); Corbis pp. 5 top (Alessandro
Della Bella/epa), 7 (Tom Bean), 8 (Ashley Cooper), 9 (Jim
Read), 11 (Robert Llewellyn), 13 (Scott Stulberg), 26
(Gene Blevins/Los Angeles Daily News); FLPA p. 17
(Hugo Binz); Getty Images pp. 4–5 (Paul and Lindamarie
Ambrose), 6 (Pete Turner), 20–21 (Pete Turner);
Imagepick p. 10 (Comstock/Jupiter Images); Ken Langford/
Mr. Random Enterprises, Inc. p. 12; NASA p. 18; Nebojsa
Kovacevic/www.unusualresearch.com p. 14; Rex Features
pp. 1 (Sipa), 20 left (Shout), 27 (Sipa); Science Photo Library
pp. 15 (Kul Bhatia), 19 (Science Source), 23 (Peter
Menzel), 24–25 (NASA); Sky Fire Productions p. 24 left;
Topfoto p. 16 (The Image Works); University of Florida
Lightning Research Group pp. 28, 29.

The front cover shows a lightning strike in Monument
Valley along the Arizona-Utah border (Getty Images/
Hans Strand).

Every effort has been made to contact copyright holders
of material reproduced in this book. Any omissions will be
rectified in subsequent printings if notice is given to the
publishers.

CONTENTS

Abbreviations m stands for meters • ft stands for feet • km stands for kilometers

Splitting the sky

It's dazzling, it's stunning and it seems to split the sky in two. But what is lightning? Have you ever wondered? If so, you're not alone.

During a storm, electricity flashes from storm clouds.

The average bolt of lightning is about 1 mile (1.6 km) long.

1 mile (1.6 km)

Lightning facts

Did you know that there are 1,800 storms happening right now? Every single second, a hundred lightning bolts zap the Earth.

energy   the ability to do work   **particles**   very tiny pieces of a substance

Millions of lightning bolts strike the Earth every year. There are many types of lightning.

A single flash of lightning contains enough **energy** to power a lightbulb for two months.

Lightning is deadly, yet beautiful. It is so powerful that it can fry a human or start a forest fire. It can also make the night sky brighter than a fireworks display on the Fourth of July.

People have been puzzling over lightning for thousands of years. Scientists are still not totally sure why it happens.

Lightning is a form of **electricity** *that may be made when water and ice* **particles collide** *inside clouds.*

MOIST AIR

electricity   the movement of charged particles to create energy

Monster sparks

When huge amounts of electricity are created in a cloud, sparks start to fly!

The biggest, most damaging lightning strikes can contain a billion **volts** of electricity! This is as much power as a **laser beam**. Laser beams can be controlled. Yet no one knows when or where lightning will strike next.

It takes an extreme type of cloud called cumulonimbus to produce lightning. With a low, flat base and a towering mass piled above, cumulonimbus clouds can be 6 miles (10 kilometers) wide and stretch the same distance into the sky.

1. Moist air is blown upward.

MOIST AIR

Record-breaking storms

Tororo in Uganda has the most thunderstorms in the world. On average, storms batter the region an astounding 251 days a year!

volt the unit used to measure the amount of electrical energy   **charge** electrical energy

2. The moisture in the rising air **freezes** and forms tiny ice crystals.

3. Cold air at the top of the cloud falls, along with raindrops and hailstones.

COLD AIR

The top of a cloud has a positive **charge**.

4. The ice, hail, and rain rub against each other and become charged with electricity.

MOIST AIR

MOIST AIR

The bottom of a cloud has a negative charge.

laser beam a narrow beam of light that is so powerful that it can cut through steel

Thunderbolts and lightning

Which is louder—a chainsaw or a thunderbolt? It's actually the thunder. A clap of thunder reaches about 120 decibels, while a chainsaw buzzes at a measly 100 decibels.

Lightning can reach sizzling temperatures, many times hotter than the surface of the Sun. This superheating creates a shockwave that is heard as thunder. Because the speed of sound is so much slower than the speed of light, thunder is always heard after lightning. It is only possible to hear thunder if you are within 10 miles (16 kilometers) of the storm itself.

This man needs ear protectors to protect his ears from the noise of the chainsaw. Thunder is even louder!

Near or far?

To work out how far away a storm is, count the seconds between a flash of lightning and the following roll of thunder. Then divide the number by 5 to get an answer in miles and by 3 to get an answer in kilometers.

decibel a unit of measurement for sound

8

Storm watchers count the time between lightning and thunder so they know how far away the storm is.

If lightning and thunder happen at almost the same time, the storm is right overhead!

Very, very frightening

The last thing you want is an exploding computer or television. That's just what can happen when lightning strikes.

Lightning doesn't need to hit your house to blow up your computer. As well as zooming along wires and pipes, a bolt of lightning sends out huge waves of energy through the air and ground. These waves can affect computers and televisions.

Don't be tempted to unplug your computer or television while a storm is overhead. Pull the plug out long before the storm arrives or stand well clear. Otherwise, you might be fried, too.

*Lightning is powerful enough to fry the delicate **circuits** inside **electronic** equipment.*

Talked to death

In the United States, most people who are killed or injured by lightning while at home are speaking on their landline telephone. Lightning can travel a long way down telephone and electrical wires. If you hear a thunderstorm, put the phone down.

circuit   a loop of electrical components that electricity flows around

Electricity travels from power stations to your home via power cables.

The power cables are strung between tall, metal towers.

If lightning hits a cable, there can be a total power failure!

electronic a device having many small parts that control an electric current, such as a TV

11

Down to Earth

When lightning zigzags from the sky, it's hard to believe that the Earth is as much to blame as the storm clouds above. Between them, the Earth and sky form a mighty team that can wreak the most terrible destruction.

Postive streamers

When negative **stepped leaders** approach the ground, **positive streamers** reach up to meet them. Once the negative and positive charges connect, there is a path between the cloud and the Earth. The lightning hurtles down this path.

The tiny spike of light to the left of this lightning bolt is a failed positive streamer.

Positive streamers connect with stepped leaders.

stepped leader   negative electric charge that zigzags downward

When negative electric charge builds up at the base of storm clouds, it needs somewhere to go. At the same time, positive electric charge builds up on Earth. The negative and positive electricity are attracted to each other.

Paths of negative electric charge **zigzag** downward.

This is a stepped leader.

The stepped leaders split and split again to form many branches.

positive streamer the part of a lightning bolt that rises from the ground

Weird lightning

All lightning hits the ground, right? Wrong! Some lightning zaps the Earth, but most leaps back and forth among the clouds.

Intracloud lightning happens between positively charged and negatively charged parts of the same cloud. Lightning that leaps between different clouds is called cloud-to-cloud lightning.

Ball lightning

Some people claim to have seen a type of lightning called "ball lightning." It is said that a ball of light flies through the air, crackling as it goes and burning objects in its path. Not everyone believes that it exists. This hasn't put scientists off trying to create ball lightning in laboratories.

Ball lightning is rarely seen, which makes it difficult to study. One theory states that it is not lightning at all.

plasma   a gas with little or no electric charge

Cloud-to-cloud lightning is usually much longer than cloud-to-ground lightning.

The bolt of lightning can **stretch** for well over 100 miles (161 km)!

Ball lightning is often confused with St. Elmo's Fire. But St. Elmo's Fire is actually **plasma** that appears as a bright blue or violet light. It glows around tall objects such as spires and masts during thunderstorms. Many say that St. Elmo's Fire happens just before lightning strikes. If you catch a glimpse, *run!*

At a distance, cloud-to-cloud lightning can be seen streaking across a stormy sky.

Bull's-eye!

You might think that taking shelter from a storm under a tree is a good way to stay dry. It might be—but it's also an excellent way to get struck by lightning.

Anything that stands above the ground level is a target for lightning. Whether it's a tree, a church spire, or a lone golfer, nothing is safe from the colossal power of a lightning strike.

The best way to stay out of danger is to follow these simple rules:

- If you are outside, look for shelter. Buildings and cars are good. Trees are *bad*.

- If there's nowhere to take shelter, make yourself as small as possible (see page 21).

- If you are inside, stay away from the phone and all plumbing pipes.

This pine tree in Colorado was struck by lightning. It burst into flames and caused a huge forest fire.

lightning rod   a metal strip or pole that allows the electricity in lightning to flow safely to Earth

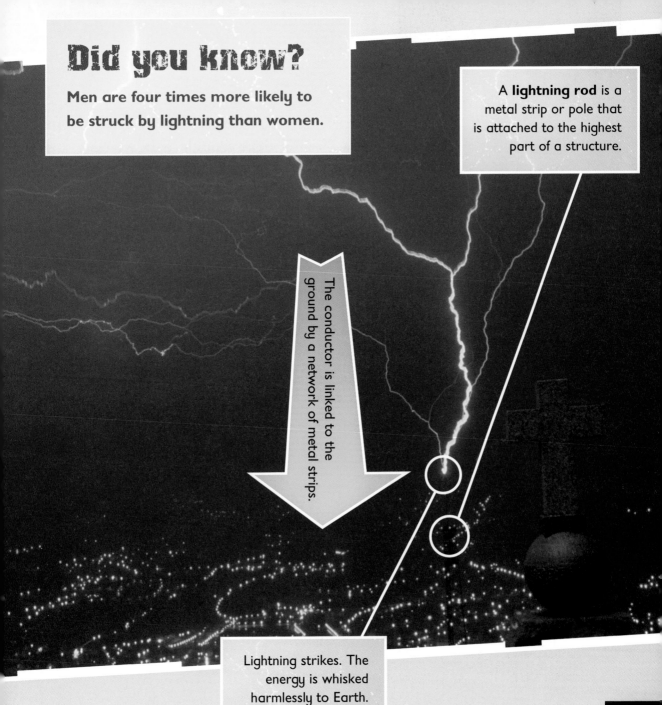

Did you know?

Men are four times more likely to be struck by lightning than women.

A **lightning rod** is a metal strip or pole that is attached to the highest part of a structure.

The conductor is linked to the ground by a network of metal strips.

Lightning strikes. The energy is whisked harmlessly to Earth.

Under attack

The movie industry suggests that astronauts are most at risk from invading aliens. The truth is even scarier. It's lightning they should really be worried about. It can stop a rocket from even leaving Earth!

Florida is the lightning capital of the entire United States. It's also where the space shuttle is launched. The launch tower and the space shuttle reach high into the air, so they are both in terrible danger of being struck by lightning.

The space shuttle on its way to the launchpad.

Lightning Alley

One part of Florida receives more lightning strikes than any other. The route between Tampa and Orlando is known as Lightning Alley, because it is struck so often.

launch pad a rocket lifts off from here

If lightning strikes, the electronics systems on board the space shuttle have to be retested before takeoff.

In 2002, a spectacular fork of lightning struck the launchpad itself.

To protect the launchpad and spacecraft from lightning, the launch tower has a tall mast perched on top.

A steel cable travels from the mast right down to the ground.

When lightning hits the mast, it flows safely down the cable and into the ground.

Zap, crackle, and pop

If you're unlucky enough to be struck by lightning, the good news is that you will probably live. Nine out of every ten people who are struck by lightning survive. The bad news is that it will hurt—a lot!

If your hair stands on end during a thunderstorm, duck! It's a sign that you might be about to be struck by lightning.

A lightning strike sends many thousands of volts of electricity through your body for a fraction of a second. This is long enough to cause burns and to zap your **nervous system**, so your muscles don't work for a while.

This man's foot was injured by a lightning strike. Ouch!

nervous system   the body's brain, spinal cord, and nerves

If you're caught out in a storm, you should never lie on the ground. The less of your body that is touching the ground, the better.

Water blow

It's a really bad idea to be sweaty or wet when you're hit by lightnin The water can explode and blow your clothes and shoes!

This woman photographing a

To keep herself as safe as possible, she crouches down with her feet close together.

She should also bend her head as low as it will go without touching the ground. Otherwise she might be

fried!

Full metal jacket

Did you know that if you're caught in a thunderstorm, the best place to be is inside a metal box or a layer of **mesh**? Whether it's an airplane or a car, the metal conducts the electricity safely away.

The driver's view of a lightning storm. Inside the car, the passengers are safe from lightning as they drive through a huge thunderstorm.

Silver, copper, gold, and mixtures of tin and lead are the best types of conductor. Electricity travels through them very quickly.

mesh crisscrossed material such as wire   **conductive** able to conduct electricity or heat

The incredible metal safety net

A **Faraday** cage (named after the scientist Michael Faraday) is any solid or meshed cage made of **conductive** material. When bolts of electricity hit the cage, it protects the equipment or people inside. It is particularly good at shielding its contents from lightning strikes.

The metal bars are close together.

When electricity hits the metal bars, it is conducted safely away.

The man inside this Faraday cage is protected from lightning strikes—so long as he doesn't touch the cage.

Faraday, Michael   a 19th-century English scientist who studied electricity and magnetism

View from space

For years, airplane pilots reported seeing something very strange during storms. They claimed that flashes appeared *above* thunderstorms, too. But no one believed them.

A sprite 30–55 miles (48–89 km) up in the air above a thunderstorm. Its true color is pinkish red.

This was until astronauts rocketed into space and saw the mysterious flashes for themselves. We now know that these bursts of light are a type of lightning. Scientists call them "sprites." They are still working out why sprites happen. Sprites last just a fraction of a second, yet they reach high into the **atmosphere**.

atmosphere   the mixture of gases that surrounds the Earth

Out of this world

Earth isn't the only planet to have lightning. Sizzling storms have been spotted in Saturn's atmosphere, too. In 2006, astronomers recorded an enormous storm there. It was larger than the United States. The lightning was a thousand times more powerful than the strikes that hit Earth.

This image of storms on Earth was taken from the International Space Station.

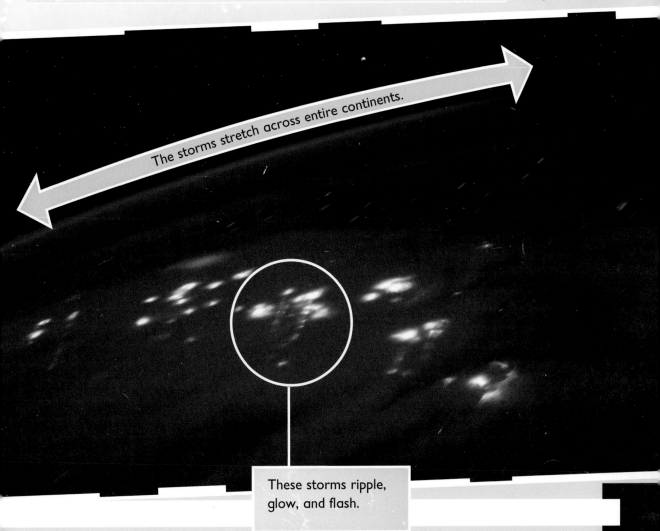

The storms stretch across entire continents.

These storms ripple, glow, and flash.

Dust demons

As if mind-bogglingly fast winds, lashing rain, and the occasional flying cow weren't enough to deal with, if you're ever caught in a **tornado**, you also run the risk of being struck by lightning!

Lightning can happen without thunderclouds. All that's needed are vast clouds of swirling particles. Next time you're watching a volcano erupt or taking shelter from a tornado or hurricane, watch out for lightning, too. It won't be far behind.

Lightning has also been spotted during really wild forest fires, nuclear explosions, and massive snowstorms.

The hurricane whips up dust, dirt, and water from the ground. If the storm clouds become charged with electricity, lightning can begin flashing around the sky.

tornado   violent storm with very strong winds that swirl in a circular motion

Early warning

Scientists believe that small bolts of lightning flash at the volcano's **vent** during eruptions. This electric charge can be detected before the eruption is spotted. In the future, planes flying nearby could be warned of the risk of lightning.

1. Volcanoes hurl out giant clouds of dust and ash.

2. When the ash particles rub together, they cause electricity.

3. The lightning starts.

vent   opening in the Earth's crust where a volcano is formed

Liftoff!

Who in their right mind would fire a rocket near a thunderstorm? A lightning scientist, that's who!

No wonder lightning is so difficult to study. It lasts just a fraction of a second, and no one knows where it will happen next. To make their job easier, scientists create their very own lightning bolts using rockets.

ZAP! Scientists triggered this lightning strike.

Flash, bang, wallop!

Some scientists think that lightning might have helped to kick-start life on Earth!

Each rocket trails a metal wire behind it. The other end of the wire is attached to the ground.

What triggers lightning? Why does it choose one path rather than another? And why does lightning travel *upward* from thunderclouds? These are just some of the mysteries that scientists hope to solve.

When the rocket flies upward, it triggers lightning at a height of about 1,000 ft (305 m).

Lightning travels down the wire.

The lightning **zaps** exactly where the scientists want it.

Glossary

atmosphere the mixture of gases that surrounds the Earth

charge electrical energy

circuit a loop of electrical components that electricity flows around

collide when things bump into one another

conductor material that electricity or heat travels along easily

decibel a unit of measurement for sound

electricity the movement of charged particles to create energy

electronic a device having many small parts that control an electric current, such as a TV

energy the ability to do work

Faraday, Michael a 19th-century English scientist who studied electricity and magnetism

laser beam a narrow beam of light that is so powerful that it can cut through steel

launchpad a rocket lifts off from here

lightning rod a metal strip or pole that allows the electricity in lightning to flow safely to Earth

mesh crisscrossed material such as wire

nervous system the body's brain, spinal cord, and nerves

particles very tiny pieces of a substance

plasma a gas with little or no electric charge

positive streamer the part of a lightning bolt that rises from the ground

stepped leader negative electric charge that zigzags downward

tornado violent storm with very strong winds that swirl in a circular motion

vent opening in the Earth's crust where a volcano is formed

volt the unit used to measure the amount of electrical energy

Further information

Books

Lightning by Seymour Simon (HarperCollins, 2006)
How different types of lightning occur, plus interesting statistics and stories.

Twisters and Other Terrible Storms (Random House Books for Young Readers, 2003)
How the Earth's weather is formed and all about the deadliest storms on Earth.

Web sites

FactHound offers a safe, fun way to find Internet sites related to this book. All of the sites on FactHound have been researched by our staff. Visit *www.facthound.com* for age-appropriate sites. You may browse subjects by clicking on letters, or by clicking on pictures and words.
FactHound will fetch the best sites for you!

Films

Lightning: Bolts of Destruction directed by Brenton Spencer (Legacy Filmworks, 2003; PG)
A family races to save the world from violent lightning storms.

The Perfect Storm directed by Wolfgang Petersen (Baltimore Spring Creek Productions, 2000; PG-13)
A true story of a monster storm that hit New England in 1991.

Index